The Powerful Ocean

Shelly C. Buchanan, M.S.

Consultant

Jill Tobin
California Teacher of the Year
Semi-Finalist
Burbank Unified School District

Publishing Credits

Rachelle Cracchiolo, M.S.Ed., *Publisher*
Conni Medina, M.A.Ed., *Managing Editor*
Diana Kenney, M.A.Ed., NBCT, *Content Director*
Dona Herweck Rice, *Series Developer*
Robin Erickson, *Multimedia Designer*
Timothy Bradley, *Illustrator*

Image Credits: p.5 Charles V. Angelo/Science Source;
Back cover iStock; p.7 Gary Hincks/Science Source; p.9
(illustration) Timothy Bradley; p.10 National Oceanic and
Atmospheric Administration, (background) Wikimedia
Commons; p.13 Alamy, (illustration) Timothy Bradley;
p.18 Danté Fenolio/Science Source; p.19 NOAA Office
of Exploration and Research; p.20 (illustration) Timothy
Bradley; p.22 Science Source; p.23 (illustration) Timothy
Bradley; p.24 Claus Lunau/Science Source; all other
images from Shutterstock.

Library of Congress Cataloging-in-Publication Data

Buchanan, Shelly, author.
  The powerful ocean / Shelly C. Buchanan.
    pages cm
  Summary: "The ocean is beautiful, powerful, and
refreshing. It's home to many amazing and unique
creatures. The salty water provides the perfect home
for many plants and animals. Within these waters are
choppy currents and strong tides. But without the ocean,
our world would be a very different place."-- Provided
by publisher.
  Audience: Grades 4 to 6
  Includes index.
  ISBN 978-1-4807-4726-5 (pbk.)
1. Ocean--Juvenile literature.
2. Oceanography--Juvenile literature.
3. Marine animals--Juvenile literature. I. Title.
  GC21.5.B83 2016
  551.46--dc23

Teacher Created Materials

5301 Oceanus Drive
Huntington Beach, CA 92649-1030
http://www.tcmpub.com

ISBN 978-1-4807-4726-5

© 2016 Teacher Created Materials, Inc.
Printed in China
Nordica.082019.CA21901409

Table of Contents

Watery World

Planet Earth is a unique place. It's the only planet in our solar system with liquid water. In fact, nearly 75 percent of the place we call home is covered in water. Scientists think water was the key to developing life here. It's a wonder we call our planet *Earth*. *Water* might be a better name!

Water takes many shapes on our home planet. Lakes, rivers, seas, and ponds give our home beautiful landscapes. But the ocean is the biggest and mightiest water feature of all. Out of all the water surrounding us, 96 percent of it is found in the ocean.

Scientists continue to make amazing discoveries in these wild waters. With the use of modern technology, scientists shed light on a hidden underwater world. There's still so much more to learn. After all, we know more about space than we know about the dark depths of our own ocean. In fact, about 500 people have been to space, but only three have reached the deepest part of the ocean.

There may be five oceans—Arctic, Atlantic, Indian, Pacific, and Southern—but it is really one massive water body: our ocean.

Investigating Big Blue

People are making many new discoveries about the ocean. Currently, there are 47 different species of sea horses that we are aware of. Just in the past eight years, scientists discovered 14 of them.

longsnout sea horse

When Earth was formed billions of years ago, it did not have water. Gases from volcanoes formed much of the water on Earth. Comets also brought water to the planet as they crashed. Over time, water filled the oceans. Millions of years ago, there was one massive ocean called *Panthalassa*. Earth's land was all connected in a mass known as *Pangaea*. The land changed and moved over time until it reached its current shape. And it continues to change slowly today.

Today, there are five oceans. Although they are given different names, they are all connected. This makes up the largest part of the **hydrosphere**. The hydrosphere refers to all the liquid water on Earth.

There are wonders beneath the surface of the great waters. Millions of years after the ocean was formed, life began in its waters. Oceans have a rich range of plant and animal life. Scientists have counted 230,000 species. But they suspect four times more than that are waiting to be discovered! There are even fascinating underwater landscapes. There is much more than meets the eye beneath the ocean's surface.

Atlantic Ocean

Pacific Ocean

The Proud Pacific!

The Pacific Ocean is by far the largest of all five oceans. It contains 28 percent of Earth's water and spans over 60 million square miles. This means it's larger than all the land on Earth put together!

Supercontinent

The world as we know it used to be one massive supercontinent. Scientists believe that Pangaea started to split because of a theory called *continental drift*. The theory states that the land split apart and drifted, forming separate continents.

Pacific Ocean

Indian Ocean

 Panthalassa comes from Greek words meaning "all ocean."

Southern Ocean

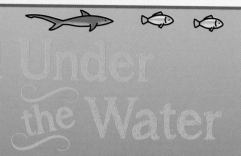

Land Under the Water

If you look at the oceans as a whole, they form large basins, or bowls, filled with water. They slope upward as they approach the continents. But there are large, flat parts in the ocean that are thousands of meters deep. As you move deeper into the ocean, there is more pressure and less light. This creates different underwater layers that provide different kinds of **habitats** for plants and animals. Each layer is broken up into its own zone.

First, there is the sunlight zone. Here, 90 percent of ocean life is found. The next layer is the twilight zone. It is cold and dark in this region, but some light still gets through. The next layer is the midnight zone. It is completely dark, and the water is almost freezing. The animals that can live here look very strange! Below that is the abyss. Here, bottom feeders can be found. Finally, the **trenches** are the lowest points on Earth. Few animals that we know of can live in this harsh environment.

●●○○ 🛜

Ocean Zones

Zone	Depth	Temperature	Wildlife
sunlight	0–200 m (0–656 ft.)	-2°–36°C (28°–97°F)	sharks, sea turtles, coral
twilight	200–1,000 m (656–3,280 ft.)	4°–13°C (39°–55°F)	jellyfish, shrimp, sea dragons, worms
midnight	1,000–4,000 m (3,280–13,120 ft.)	4°C (39°F)	algae, anglerfish, lantern fish, squid
abyss	4,000–6,000 m (13,120–19,685 ft.)	2°–3°C (36°–37°F)	sea urchins, sea lilies, giant squid
trenches	6,000+ m (19,685+ ft.)	1°–3°C (34°–37°F)	Scientists just recently began studies here.

sunlight zone

 twilight zone

midnight zone

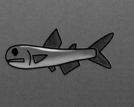

Exploring Mariana

Challenger Deep is the deepest part of the Mariana Trench and the deepest spot in the ocean. At more than 11,000 meters (36,000 feet) deep, it is deeper than Mt. Everest is tall! There have only been four expeditions to reach Challenger Deep. Jacques Piccard and Don Walsh were the first to reach it in 1960.

abyss

 The trenches are sometimes called the *hadal zone.* It is named after Hades, the Greek god of the underworld.

trenches

The underwater landscapes are as varied as those above. There are vast, flat plains; massive mountain ranges; and wide valleys. These formations continue to develop and change. This is because Earth's crust, or outer layer, shifts.

The crust is made up of large sections of rock called **tectonic plates**. These plates slowly move and shift. It took about 230 million years for Earth to create the continents we are familiar with today. Where tectonic plates meet, they create mountains, volcanoes, and deep ocean trenches.

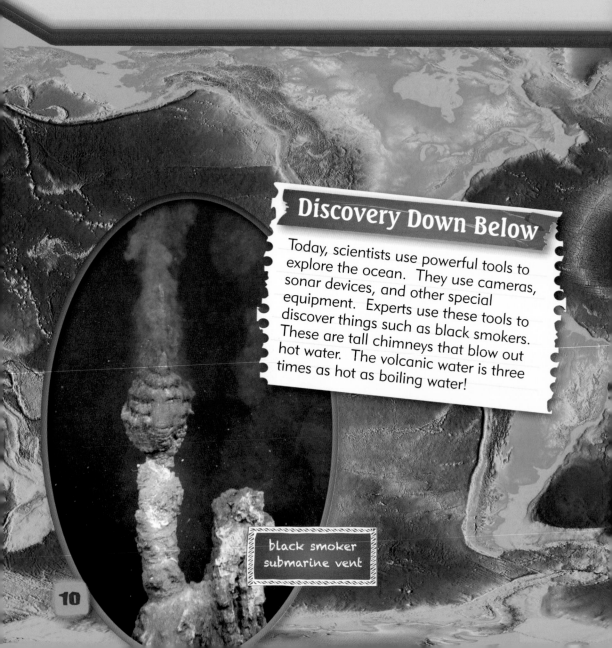

Discovery Down Below

Today, scientists use powerful tools to explore the ocean. They use cameras, sonar devices, and other special equipment. Experts use these tools to discover things such as black smokers. These are tall chimneys that blow out hot water. The volcanic water is three times as hot as boiling water!

black smoker
submarine vent

The ground below the water, closest to the shore is the **continental shelf**. It is the edge of the land or continent that lies under ocean water. On average, these shelves are 65 kilometers (40 miles) wide. Most are around 61 m (200 ft.) deep. A few are more than 149 m (489 ft.) deep. Since this is in the sunlight zone of the ocean, there is an abundance of marine life. Many familiar sea animals and plants live in or visit this area.

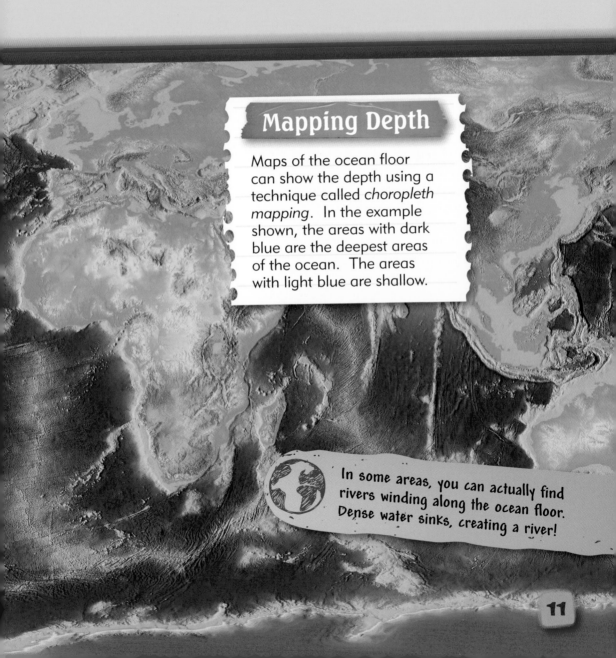

Mapping Depth

Maps of the ocean floor can show the depth using a technique called *choropleth mapping*. In the example shown, the areas with dark blue are the deepest areas of the ocean. The areas with light blue are shallow.

In some areas, you can actually find rivers winding along the ocean floor. Dense water sinks, creating a river!

Moving out from the continental shelf, the ocean floor quickly drops off into cold darkness. This drop-off is the **continental slope**, and it extends thousands of meters. At the bottom, we find the **abyssal plain**. This large, flat area makes up the bottom of the ocean basin. These huge plains make up 54 percent of Earth's surface. Plain areas are broken up in places by craggy cliffs and deep trenches. The shifting of tectonic plates creates these spectacular underwater features.

Plates that pull apart allow hot lava to slowly ooze out of the ground, making underwater mountain chains. Some are active volcanoes that erupt with a red-hot spew of lava. Some grow so huge that they break the surface of the water. Many become reefs and islands.

When plates crash together, one may be pushed below the other. Part of the crust is dragged beneath Earth's crust. This forms deep trenches where few have explored.

Although oceans are like giant bowls, they are not smooth like the ones in our kitchen cupboards. They have bumps, ridges of mountains, and plunging trenches. Under the ocean's waters, we find a world as complex as the one above.

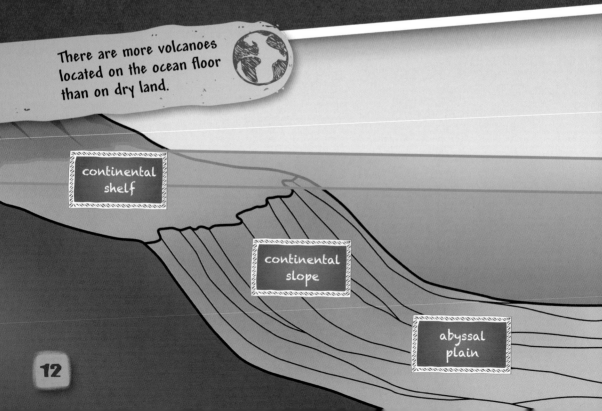

There are more volcanoes located on the ocean floor than on dry land.

continental shelf

continental slope

abyssal plain

Into the Darkness

The continental slope has freezing temperatures, high pressure, and almost no visible light. The animals that call this place home have some unusual characteristics that allow them to thrive in this harsh environment. Most of the organisms have dark colors, unlike their shallow-living pals. This is because it is extremely dark in this part of the ocean.

Wolf fish

Measuring from the base of the ocean floor to its peak, Mauna Kea in Hawaii is the tallest mountain in the world at 10,203 m (33,476 ft.) tall.

Mauna Kea summit

Ocean Life

Earth's oceans are teeming with life. They range from **microscopic** plants to enormous blue whales. You are probably familiar with some kind of ocean life. But there are many other life forms that will amaze you. Have you heard of the flamingo tongue snail or the vampire squid? Scientists report there are still many ocean plants and animals yet to be discovered!

flamingo
tongue
snails

Making Friends

In La Jolla (luh HOI-uh), California, near the caves in the water, you can find harbor seals. These seals are very playful when in the water, and the babies have even been known to get into the kayaks of people nearby! These shoreline creatures sometimes need a rest while they are in the water.

Marine Iguana

Only one kind of iguana lives near the ocean—the marine iguana from the Galapagos Islands. This dragon-like creature dives into the ocean from the warm island rocks. Here, it feasts on seaweed. For maximum dining pleasure, this iguana can hold its breath for up to 20 minutes!

Shoreline

The shoreline habitat is where the ocean meets land. These areas can be rocky, sandy, or marshy. They are home to a wide range of creatures able to adapt to the rising and falling **tides**.

On sandy shores, you might see shellfish such as snails, hermit crabs, and razor clams. You might see coastal birds such as seagulls and cranes hunting for these tasty morsels. Rocky shores are home to plants and animals with an iron grip. They are able to withstand waves crashing on boulders and rocks. Here you will find strong seaweed with root-like suckers that keep them planted on rocks. Animals such as sea anemones, barnacles, and sea stars have adapted for survival in tide pools. These plants and animals thrive despite being thrashed by waves.

Coral Reefs

Coral reefs are home to one fourth of the ocean's plants and animals. These special habitats are found mainly in tropical regions. Corals are animals that create these beautiful reefs. They build tough outer skeletons. Live corals provide housing and shelter for plants and other animals.

Octopuses, sea horses, moray eels, and many other species enjoy these warm-water habitats. Sharks and barracuda visit these areas in search of prey.

For Your Eyes Only!

If you are ever lucky enough to visit a coral reef, enjoy it with your eyes only. Touching the reef will damage it. Be sure to stay off the seafloor. Swirling sediment from the bottom will smother coral. Be careful and respect this tropical wonder!

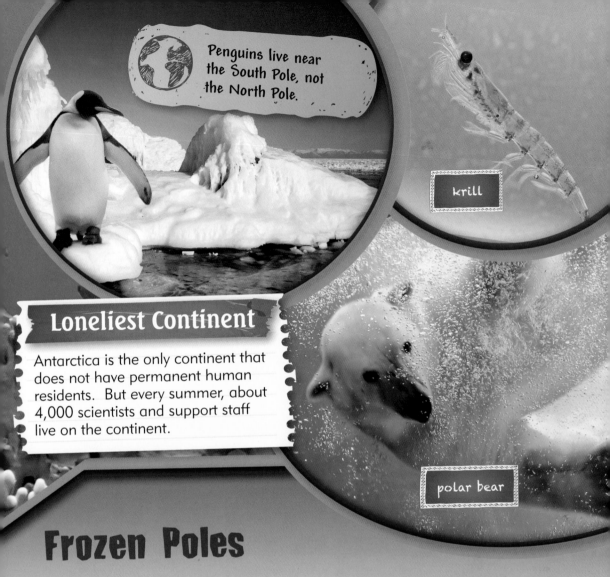

Penguins live near the South Pole, not the North Pole.

krill

Loneliest Continent

Antarctica is the only continent that does not have permanent human residents. But every summer, about 4,000 scientists and support staff live on the continent.

polar bear

Frozen Poles

Much of Earth's poles are locked in ice. The ocean temperatures drop below freezing during dark winter months. Then, there is nonstop sunshine in the summer.

Many **polar** animals pack on fat. This helps them maintain adequate body heat. They carry thick layers of blubber under their skin. They stay cozy in the winter months. Healthy polar bears, walruses, and whales are all pleasantly plump!

Polar water is loaded with nutrients. Such food supports life in these harsh habitats. Tiny creatures called *krill* live in groups of millions. They are a main source of food for many polar animals.

Wide Open Ocean

Most of the ocean is open water far from the shoreline and ocean floor. The top sunlight zone of open water holds most ocean life. Life here starts with phytoplankton. They are at the bottom of the food chain. These tiny plants use the sun's energy to grow. Microscopic zooplankton and other ocean animals eat phytoplankton. Jellyfish, seals, whales, and others love to dine on these microscopic delights. Sharks and other large fish hunt here, too.

While scientists have conducted large amounts of research on the sunlight zone, little research has been done in the twilight zone due to lack of light. There isn't even enough light for plants to live there. Animals that live in this zone must be able to withstand great pressure. The giant squid calls this home. Some whales dive down to this zone to hunt. They must hold their breath for up to 20 minutes at a time.

Bioluminescent Beasts

Some deep-ocean dwellers such as the lantern fish are bioluminescent. These creatures have light-producing organs called *photophores* on their heads, tails, or underbellies. They do this to lure prey and attract mates.

lantern fish

Do You Sea the Ocean?

The Sargasso Sea is located in the middle of the Atlantic Ocean. Unlike most seas, it isn't surrounded by land— it's surrounded by more water! The sea is its own small ecosystem. Floating Sargassum seaweed covers the surface of the sea and provides food and shelter for the organisms living here.

Sargassum seaweed

Down Deep and Dark

Below 1,000 m (3,280 ft.), the water is completely dark. This is the midnight zone. Here, the predators are fierce. They have huge eyes, spiky teeth, and sharp fins.

Near the very bottom live truly unusual creatures, such as the anglerfish and the tripod fish. Many are totally blind. After all, who needs eyes when it's pitch black?

Ocean Motion

Ocean water is always on the move. Ocean water moves in **currents** and tides. Water is pulled back from the shore and then returns later. Many forces are at work to create this movement.

Currents

Ocean currents are powerful streams of water. They travel like great rivers under the surface of the water. Currents are created by wind, gravity, the rotation of Earth, and temperature. These forces move water hundreds and thousands of miles. This movement stirs up nutrients from the ocean floor for sea life to eat. Currents also move the sun's heat through ocean waters. This helps regulate ocean and land temperatures.

Waves

Waves form out in open water. Wind pushes against the water and causes it to ripple. These waves continue to move through the water until they get near land. As the water gets shallow, the bottom of the wave slows, but the top doesn't. This makes the wave trip over itself and crash.

ripples

waves

sand

low tide

Tides

The moon is largely responsible for ocean tides. Its gravity pulls at the ocean as it revolves around Earth. This causes sea levels to rise and fall twice each and every day. But the sun also plays a part. The sun's gravity is much stronger, but it is also farther away from Earth. When the sun and moon pull in the same direction, tides are more extreme. But when their gravity pulls in opposite directions, tides don't rise or fall as much.

high tide

Hydrologic Cycle

No matter where you live in the world, Earth's water affects you. The water cycle, or **hydrologic cycle**, is part of the world's weather systems. It's responsible for circulating water around the globe.

The sun warms Earth's surfaces. This energy causes liquid water to **evaporate** and turn into water vapor. Water vapor **condenses** into droplets and forms clouds. Wind blows the clouds all around the world. When clouds gather enough water, **precipitation** falls to the ground. It may take the form of rain, snow, sleet, or hail depending on the conditions. This sends water back to Earth's surface. Some of the water soaks into the ground. But most runs downhill into rivers and streams, which flow to the ocean.

The ocean's temperature and currents make some places warmer and others cooler. The ocean also provides water that precipitates back down, distributing water around the globe. Without all this water movement, the world would be a very different place.

Salty Rain?

You may be wondering why rainwater isn't salty if it comes from the ocean. When water evaporates, it turns into a gas. The gas can't take the salt with it, so the salt stays behind. Only fresh, salt-free water from the ocean forms clouds.

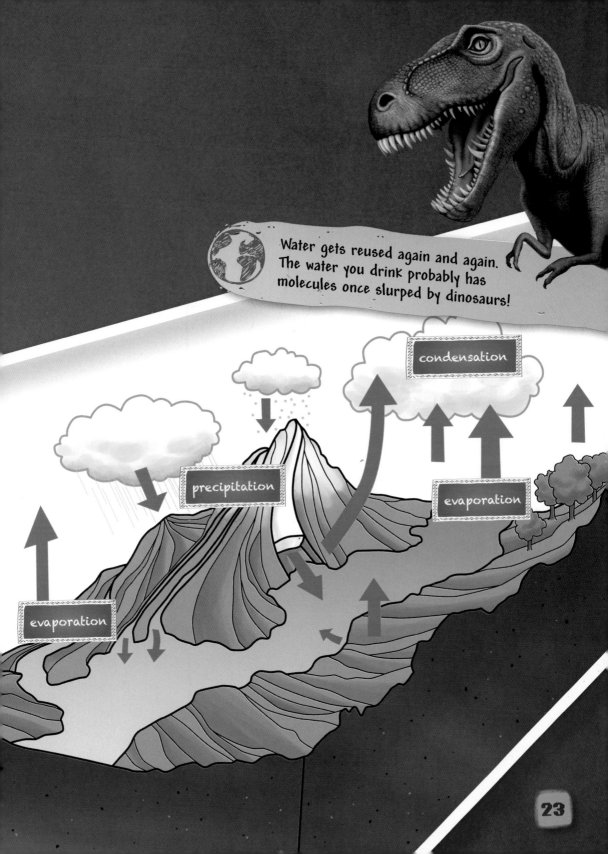

Water gets reused again and again. The water you drink probably has molecules once slurped by dinosaurs!

condensation

precipitation

evaporation

evaporation

Climate Connections

Climate is the long-term pattern of weather conditions in a region. The ocean helps regulate the world's climate. It's a delicate balance. Without it, entire ecosystems could be altered or destroyed.

Have you ever stood barefoot outside on a hot day? The scorching ground quickly burns your feet. But then, you dip your feet into a nice cool pool. Both the ground and pool have been sitting out in the sun, but it takes much more energy to heat the water, so it stays cooler. Once water is heated, it takes a long time to cool down.

Now think about all of that water in the ocean. It helps regulate temperatures worldwide. Without it, we would have scorching heat during the day and freezing cold temperatures at night. Life may not even be possible in such conditions. You may live far away from the ocean, but it still affects the climate in your area.

El Niño

El Niño is the abnormal warming of the surface water of the eastern Pacific Ocean. It occurs about every five years. El Niño generally causes drier conditions *(sun symbols)* in Australia and southeast Asia, and wetter and warmer conditions *(raindrop symbols)* in the Americas.

Releasing CO$_2$

Oceans also decrease Earth's temperature by absorbing portions of carbon dioxide (CO$_2$) from the atmosphere. Carbon dioxide helps keep heat in the atmosphere. But, when the ocean absorbs carbon dioxide, less heat is trapped.

Protecting the Ocean

Our mighty ocean is home to a wide and wild range of sea life. Scientists haven't even discovered the half of it yet. We do know that the ocean is a key player in maintaining all life on Earth. It is critical for our survival.

Scientists know that our ocean is in danger. Garbage, industrial waste, oil spills, and sewage are polluting ocean water. This pollution is killing sea life. What it does not kill, it poisons. Huge garbage patches float in open water. These polluted areas are choking animals. There are also massive oil slicks suffocating fish and birds.

Many fishing companies use high-tech equipment and overfish the water. They take fish out of the ocean faster than the supply can be replenished.

Together we can learn how to take care of the powerful and important ocean. Tell your family and friends to get involved. Even recycling can make a big difference.

Go Green...or, Blue

Everyone can make a difference, and it starts with you. Here are a few simple steps to reaching that goal:

- Use reusable bottles instead of plastic.
- Always dispose of harmful materials properly.
- Pick up your trash. Leave places nicer than when you got there.
- Educate others. Share what you learn about the ocean.

 Recycling plastic or not using plastic at all can decrease ocean pollution by 80 percent!

Think Like a Scientist

How do the atmosphere and water interact? Experiment and find out!

What to Get

- large glass bowl
- plastic wrap
- small bowl or cup
- small rock or weight
- water

What to Do

1 Fill a large bowl with a few centimeters of water. Place the small bowl in the center of the large bowl.

2 Cover the large bowl with plastic wrap. Place a small rock or weight on top of the plastic wrap, centered over the smaller bowl.

3 Place the bowl in a sunny location. Check back in a few hours. What do you observe? What do you think caused this?

Glossary

abyssal plain—large, flat area of land on the ocean floor

climate—the usual type of weather a place gets

condenses—changes from a gas to a liquid

continental shelf—the part of a continent that lies under the ocean and slopes down to the ocean floor

continental slope—the steep slope from a continental shelf to the ocean floor

currents—continual movements of water or air in the same direction

evaporate—to change from a liquid to a gas

habitats—places where particular plants or animals live

hydrologic cycle—the cycle by which water continuously circulates from Earth to the atmosphere and back to Earth

hydrosphere—all the water in the atmosphere and on the surface of Earth

microscopic—extremely small object, so small that it can only be seen with a microscope

polar—of or relating to the North or South Pole or the region around it

precipitation—water that falls to the ground as rain, snow, sleet, or hail

tectonic plates—giant pieces of Earth's crust that move

tides—rising and falling of the surface water due to the gravitational pull of the sun and moon

trenches—long, narrow ditches in the ocean floor

Index

A Little Goes a Long Way

Water is all around us. Observe water at different stages in the
water cycle. Look carefully for dew on blades of grass. Carefully
study a puddle after a rainstorm. Observe frost on a window. What do
you notice? What stage of the water cycle are you observing? What